Hidden surprise CAKES

CONTENTS

INTRODUCTION

It's the latest baking trend sweeping the Internet and one that will have everyone gasping in amazement. Using a variety of clever techniques we've created a selection of sensational cakes and cupcakes that look just like any other on the outside, but as soon as you cut a slice from a cake or bite into a cupcake a delightful hidden surprise is revealed. From a mighty multi-coloured layered Rainbow Cake to a Piñata Party Cake bursting with sweets, a spiced Halloween loaf with a black sponge bat in each slice or a frosted cupcake fizzing with popping candy, there's a cake here for every occasion. Some are quick and easy to make, while others need a little more time and skill, but each recipe has clear and concise instructions with detailed step-by-step pictures to guide you. These cakes are fun to make and will certainly keep everyone guessing – it's up to you whether you give away the secret!

TECHNIQUES

HIDDEN SPONGE SHAPE CAKES

Although time-consuming to make, these cakes really do have the ultimate wow factor! The technique is quite simple, if a little fiddly, but once you've perfected it you can experiment with a whole variety of different themed shapes and colours. Cleverly created by concealing a row or circle of ready-baked sponge shapes within the sponge cake mixture before baking, the two secrets to success are to keep the shaped sponge design fairly simple and to make sure that the shapes are placed as closely together as possible when they go back in the tin for the final bake. The stunning Polka Dot Cake on page 46 and the Hidden Heart Cupcakes on page 68 are the easiest cakes to make using this method, so perhaps try one of these recipes first.

LAYERED OR PATTERNED SPONGE CAKES

Colouring sponge mixture is an effective way to create impact for a special celebration cake. From layered rainbow colours to subtle shaded ombre cakes they are quite easy to make. You will find that batter is able to take plenty of food colouring – after baking the surface of the sponges may be a little moister than usual but this won't affect the taste of the finished cake. To create a patterned cake, such as the Chocolate Surprise Cake on page 16, different colours or flavours of mixture are piped into the tin before baking. The pattern will be different every time, but that makes them even more fun to bake!

CHEQUERBOARD DESIGN

Accurate cutting and careful reassembly is needed to give this style of cake a professional finish. Once you've perfected the basic technique try experimenting with different colour or flavour combinations.

CAKES WITH GOODIES INSIDE

Children will be delighted to find sweets, chocolates or popping candy inside cakes and cupcakes and this simple technique can be used to make more sophisticated cakes too, such as the Tumbling Berries Gateau on page 58. These filled cakes are best baked a day or two in advance, then filled and decorated on the day of serving.

BASIC CAKE MIXTURES

Most of the cakes in this book are based on a classic Victoria sponge cake mixture made with self-raising flour, butter, sugar and eggs. Some are made using the all-in-one method, where all the ingredients are beaten together until pale and creamy. As a general rule all-in-one cakes have a little extra baking powder added, but to avoid the layered cakes being too domed this has been omitted from some recipes.

Where a firmer mixture is needed to hold the hidden sponge shapes in place, a Madeira-style cake mixture is used. These cakes need to be cooked at a lower temperature and for quite a bit longer than usual. To check if they are cooked all the way through, gently push the skewer right down to the base of the cake, avoiding the area where the baked sponge shapes are placed.

ESSENTIAL EQUIPMENT

As well as all the usual baking paraphernalia, such as bowls, spoons, sieves, measuring spoons, jugs, baking paper and paper cupcake cases, here's a brief guide to some of the more vital pieces of equipment you will need to create these stunning cakes.

CAKE TINS

It's worth investing in a selection of good quality cake tins that will last for years. Loose-based ones make light work of removing the baked cakes from the tins. Many of the cakes in this book are made in shallow sandwich/sponge tins ranging from (15–20 cm/6–8 inches in diameter). These are the most popular sizes available and you may already have a couple of each size. For cakes that have more than two layers simply bake in batches, cleaning, re-greasing and re-lining the tins each time – or just borrow a couple of extra tins from a friend. To avoid wonky cakes, do make sure the tins you use are all exactly the same size!

SILICONE MOULDS

Silicone bakeware is flexible, lightweight and easy to store and clean, but the range of sizes is not as extensive as it is for metal bakeware. However, to make the Polka Dot Cake on page 46, you will need a couple of deep round cake moulds and a cake pop mould, and for the Birthday Surprise Giant Cupcake on page 74, you'll need a giant cupcake silicone mould. You should be able to find all the moulds online or in large department stores or kitchenware retailers. Thoroughly clean the moulds in warm soapy water and make sure they are completely dry before storing.

SCALES

A good set of scales is a must when making any cakes. As well as ensuring that the ingredients are measured accurately, many of the recipes in this book will require the sponge mixture to be divided equally to ensure perfectly proportioned layers. Battery-powered digital scales that can be re-set to zero are the easiest to use.

ELECTRIC MIXER

Although this is not completely essential, few of us will make a cake nowadays without the help of a time-saving electric mixer! A hand-held one with 2–3 speed settings is ideal. A free-standing mixer will be pricier but will give you time to get on with other preparations and is especially useful for all-in-one sponge mixtures and making large quantities of buttercream.

SPATULAS

A selection of flexible silicone spatulas is ideal for dividing quantities of mixtures into separate bowls without any wastage.

PALETTE KNIVES

For the perfect finish to filled and frosted cakes, a long, flexible palette knife is essential. A smaller straight or angled palette knife will also be useful when gently smoothing cake mixture around sponge shapes.

PIPING BAGS AND NOZZLES

Large disposable polythene piping bags are reasonably priced and save time when piping swirls and rosettes on cakes and cupcakes. They also come in handy for some of the recipes where the cake mixture is piped evenly around the sponge shapes. Large or medium star-shaped nozzles are required for the swirls and rosettes and a medium-sized plain nozzle will be needed for piping cake mixture. For intricate fine piping, make a small piping bag from a triangular sheet of baking paper.

CUTTERS

A selection of round metal cutters in various sizes will be useful for cutting and decorating cakes. For cakes that have a shaped sponge inside you'll need to buy a specific cutter, such as a palm tree or heart shape. Cake decorating specialist suppliers usually have a good range of shapes and sizes. Make sure that the shaped cutter is not too large and will fit comfortably inside the cake tin.

WORKING WITH FOOD COLOURINGS

Many of the really amazing creations in this book, such as the Rainbow Cake on page 12 and the Tropical Sunrise Cake on page 60, are made with coloured sponge mixtures. To give the mixture a good strong colour without affecting the consistency it's best to use edible colouring pastes or gels. These are available in a whole kaleidoscope of colours, from pale pastels to bright primaries!

Add the colouring sparingly at first and mix in gently but thoroughly to avoid any streaks in the baked cake. You'll find the cakes that need a good strong colour will take quite a lot of paste or gel, but try not to overbeat the sponge mixture or the baked cake will have a dense and heavy texture.

FROSTINGS

Nearly all the cakes in this book are decorated with one of these quick and easy frostings in varying quantities.

>> BUTTERCREAM

This classic sweet buttery frosting is easy to work with and is perfect for sandwiching together and decorating sponge cakes. Simply made using softened butter and icing sugar and flavoured with vanilla, it will keep for up to a week in the refrigerator.
This recipe makes 1 quantity (525 g/1 lb 3 oz).

Ingredients

175 g/6 oz unsalted butter, softened
350 g/12 oz icing sugar
1 tsp vanilla extract
1 tbsp hot water

1. Place the butter in a large bowl and beat with a hand-held electric mixer for 2–3 minutes until very soft and pale.

2. Sift in half the icing sugar and mix with a wooden spoon until blended with the butter. Sift in the remaining icing sugar and mix again.

3. Add the vanilla extract and beat for 2–3 minutes, or until the mixture is very smooth, pale and creamy. Add the hot water and beat for a further 30 seconds to give the buttercream a silky smooth texture.

VARIATIONS

Chocolate: Blend 2 tablespoons of cocoa powder with 2 tablespoons of boiling water to make a smooth paste. Leave to cool for a few minutes, then beat into the buttercream.

Almond: Replace the vanilla extract with almond extract.

Lemon or orange: Replace the vanilla extract with 2 tablespoons of lemon juice or orange juice. Add some finely grated lemon zest or orange zest to the buttercream, if liked.

TIP

To colour buttercream, add a little food colouring paste or gel with the tip of a cocktail stick and beat in thoroughly to give an even colour.

>> GLOSSY CHOCOLATE FROSTING

Rich, smooth and intensely chocolatey, this frosting has a wonderful glossy finish and spreads well. Use a good quality plain chocolate with 50–70% cocoa solids. This recipe makes 1 quantity (375 g/13 oz).

Ingredients

175 g/6 oz plain chocolate, broken into pieces
100 g/3½ oz butter, diced
100 ml/3½ fl oz double cream

1. Put the chocolate and butter in a large heatproof bowl. Set the bowl over a saucepan of simmering water, making sure the base of the bowl doesn't touch the water, and heat until the chocolate and butter have melted.

2. Remove the bowl from the heat and stir the mixture until smooth. Leave to cool for 2–3 minutes, then stir in the cream. Leave to stand at room temperature for 20–30 minutes, then chill in the refrigerator for 40–50 minutes, stirring occasionally, until thick enough to spread.

VARIATIONS

Mocha: Dissolve 1 teaspoon of coffee granules in 1 tablespoon of boiling water. Leave to cool, then add to the heatproof bowl with the chocolate and diced butter.
Mint: Stir a few drops of peppermint extract into the melted mixture with the cream.
Orange: Add ½–1 teaspoon of pure orange extract to the melted mixture with the cream.

>> CREAM CHEESE FROSTING

This tangy frosting has a lovely smooth, light consistency and is perfect for spreading over rich chocolate cakes or piping in generous swirls on top of cupcakes. It will keep in the refrigerator for a couple of days. This recipe makes 1 quantity (280 g/10 oz).

Ingredients

115 g/4 oz full-fat soft cheese

55 g/2 oz unsalted butter, softened

½ tsp vanilla extract

115 g/4 oz icing sugar, sifted

1. Put the soft cheese and butter in a bowl and beat together with a wooden spoon until smooth and thoroughly blended.

2. Beat in the vanilla extract, then sift in the icing sugar and beat again until the frosting is smooth and creamy. Chill in the refrigerator until required.

VARIATIONS

Orange or lemon: Replace the vanilla extract with 1 teaspoon of orange juice or lemon juice and add 2 teaspoons of finely grated orange zest or lemon zest, if liked.

>> MASCARPONE CREAM FROSTING

This delicious frosting has a lovely texture and goes perfectly with fresh fruit. This recipe makes 1 quantity (450 g/1 lb).

Ingredients

250 g/9 oz mascarpone cheese

25 g/1 oz icing sugar, sifted

200 ml/7 fl oz double cream

1. Place the mascarpone cheese in a large bowl and beat with a wooden spoon until very smooth.

2. Beat in the icing sugar, then gradually beat in the cream.

VARIATIONS

Lemon: Add 2 teaspoons of finely grated lemon zest and a few drops of lemon extract.

Coffee: Beat in 2 teaspoons of coffee and chicory extract with the cream.

DECORATING TIPS AND TECHNIQUES

Once you've created your special surprise-inside cake it's definitely worth taking a little time to apply the frosting and decorations. Follow these top tips to achieve the perfect finish every time.

Chilling cakes in the refrigerator or the freezer for a short while will help to give a firm cake to work on. It won't affect the flavour or texture of the cake as long as you bring the cake back to room temperature before serving.

Before you start, make sure that the frosting is the correct consistency. If it's too soft to hold its shape, chill it in the refrigerator for a little while. If it's too firm it will be difficult to spread smoothly, so you'll need to leave it at room temperature to soften slightly.

Spreading an initial, very thin layer of buttercream or cream cheese frosting onto the cake, sometimes called a 'crumb coat', will help to seal in any loose crumbs. Use a palette knife and don't worry if the cake looks a bit messy – after chilling the coated cake you'll apply a thicker layer of frosting, which will cover any crumbs and imperfections. Wipe the palette knife frequently to avoid getting crumbs in the bowl of frosting.

Be generous when applying the thicker layer of frosting and work quickly. For a smooth finish hold the palette knife almost flat to the side of the cake and use a sweeping motion all around the cake (using a cake turntable will help you to get a really smooth finish). To add texture, use the tip of the palette knife to create swirls or ridges around the side and top of the cake.

Piping swirls of frosting on cakes and cupcakes is a quick and easy way to decorate cakes and looks really impressive. If you haven't piped before make up some extra frosting and have a practice run before you start on the cake. To pipe large swirls, pipe 2–3 decreasing circles of frosting, gently lifting the piping bag as you go. For rosettes or rose swirls, start piping from the centre and pipe 2–3 circles in a tight spiral pattern close to the surface of the cake or cupcake.

STORAGE

Cakes that are filled and frosted with buttercream or glossy chocolate frosting will keep well in an airtight container in a cool place (not the refrigerator) for 3–4 days.

Cakes with a cream cheese frosting or fresh cream coating will need to be kept in the refrigerator and are best eaten within 2 days. Remove from the refrigerator 20–30 minutes before serving.

Cakes that have sweets or fruits hidden inside them are best eaten on the day of filling, although the sponges can be made 2–3 days in advance.

All the plain sponges will freeze well for up to 1 month. Make sure they are completely cold before wrapping in foil. Thaw at room temperature before filling and frosting.

RAINBOW CAKE

This cake has the ultimate 'wow' factor with a kaleidoscope of rainbow coloured sponges all smothered in sweet vanilla buttercream. It's the perfect party cake.

Serves 12–14 >> **Prep time:** 50 mins, plus time to cool & chill >> **Cooking time:** 40–44 mins

Red, orange & yellow sponges

250 g/9 oz self-raising flour

¼ tsp baking powder

250 g/9 oz butter, softened, plus extra for greasing

250 g/9 oz caster sugar

5 large eggs

red, orange and yellow food colouring pastes or gels

Green, blue & violet sponges

250 g/9 oz self-raising flour

¼ tsp baking powder

250 g/9 oz butter, softened, plus extra for greasing

250 g/9 oz caster sugar

5 large eggs

green, blue and violet food colouring pastes or gels

To decorate

2 quantities of buttercream (see page 8)

2 tsp rainbow coloured sugar sprinkles

You will also need

3 x 20-cm/8-inch round sandwich tins

1. Preheat the oven to 180°C/350°F/Gas Mark 4. Grease 3 x 20-cm/8-inch round sandwich tins and base-line with baking paper.

2. To make the red, orange and yellow sponges, sift together the flour and baking powder into a large bowl and add the butter, sugar and eggs. Beat with a hand-held electric mixer for 1–2 minutes until smooth and creamy. Weigh the mixture and divide equally into 3 separate bowls.

3. Beat enough red, orange and yellow food colouring paste into each bowl of mixture to give a good strong colour (see step pic 3).

4. Spoon the mixtures into the prepared tins and gently level the surfaces. Bake in the preheated oven for 20–22 minutes, or until risen and just firm to the touch. Leave to cool in the tins for 10 minutes, then turn out onto a wire rack and leave to cool completely. Do not switch off the oven.

5. Clean the tins, then grease them and base-line with baking paper. Make and bake the green, blue and violet sponges in the same way as you did the red, yellow and orange sponges.

6. To decorate, spread 5 tablespoons of buttercream on each of the sponges except the red one. Place the violet sponge on a board and then carefully stack the remaining sponges on top, finishing with the red sponge (see step pic 6).

P.T.O.

3

6

7

8

13

7. Spread some of the buttercream in a thin layer around the sides and over the top of the cake. Chill the cake in the refrigerator for 30 minutes (see step pic 7).

8. Spread the remaining buttercream around the sides and top of the cake, smoothing the sides with a palette knife (see step pic 8). Make slight ridges in the buttercream on the top of the cake with the tip of the palette knife, then scatter over the sugar sprinkles.

Tip

Be bold when adding the food colouring to the separate sponge mixtures to achieve a really vibrant coloured cake.

CHOCOLATE SURPRISE CAKE

Take a slice from this demure looking cake to reveal a surprise all chocoholics will love – a chocolate flavoured pattern running through it!

Serves **8** >> *Prep time:* 1 hour, plus time to cool >> *Cooking time:* 30–35 mins

2 tbsp cocoa powder

2 tbsp hot water

250 g/9 oz self-raising flour

250 g/9 oz butter, softened, plus extra for greasing

250 g/9 oz caster sugar

5 large eggs

1 tsp vanilla extract

2 tbsp milk

To decorate

1 quantity pink buttercream (see page 8)

2 tsp plain chocolate flakes

You will also need

2 x 18-cm/7-inch round sandwich tins

large disposable piping bag fitted with a large plain nozzle

2 x small disposable piping bags

1. Preheat the oven to 180°C/350°F/Gas Mark 4. Grease 2 x 18-cm/7-inch round sandwich tins and base-line with baking paper.

2. Mix the cocoa powder with the water in a small bowl to make a smooth paste and set aside. Sift the flour into a large bowl and add the butter, sugar, eggs and vanilla extract. Beat with a hand-held electric mixer for 1–2 minutes until smooth and creamy.

3. Put 115 g/4 oz of the vanilla mixture into a separate bowl and beat in 1 teaspoon of the chocolate paste to give a pale brown colour. Put a further 225 g/8 oz of the vanilla mixture into a second bowl and beat in the remaining cocoa paste to give a dark brown colour. Beat the milk into the remaining vanilla mixture (see step pic 3).

4. Spread a thin layer of the milk vanilla mixture in the base of each prepared tin and gently level the surface with a palette knife (see step pic 4). Spoon the remaining milk vanilla mixture into a large disposable piping bag fitted with a large plain nozzle. Spoon the two coloured mixtures into smaller disposable piping bags and snip off the ends.

5. Pipe some of the dark brown mixture into each prepared tin in two concentric rings, each about 2.5 cm/1 inch wide. Pipe a thinner line of light brown mixture along the centre of each dark brown ring (see step pic 5).

P.T.O.

6. Pipe the remaining dark brown mixture over the light brown mixture to cover it as much as possible (see step pic 6).

7. Pipe the remaining vanilla mixture in between the chocolate rings and evenly over the top, then gently level the surfaces with a palette knife (see step pic 7).

8. Bake in the preheated oven for 30–35 minutes, or until risen, golden and just firm to the touch. Leave to cool in the tins for 10 minutes, then turn out onto a wire rack and leave to cool completely.

9. To decorate, sandwich the two sponges together with some of the buttercream and spread the remainder around the sides and over the top of the cake, smoothing and swirling it with a palette knife (see step pic 9). Sprinkle over the chocolate flakes.

Tip

Don't worry if your piping of the two chocolate mixtures is a bit erratic – the pattern does not need to be too uniform and will probably be different each time you make it.

LADYBIRD CUPCAKES

Bite inside these cute ladybird cupcakes and you'll find a brightly coloured red sponge dotted with delicious chocolate spots!

Makes 12 >> **Prep time:** 40 mins, plus time to cool >> **Cooking time:** 20–25 mins

115 g/4 oz butter, softened

115 g/4 oz caster sugar

2 eggs, beaten

115 g/4 oz self-raising flour

¼ tsp baking powder

red food colouring paste or gel

55 g/2 oz plain chocolate chips

To decorate

1 quantity green buttercream (see page 8)

115 g/4 oz red ready-to-roll icing

55 g/2 oz black ready-to-roll icing

boiled water, cooled

tubes of black and white writing icing

You will also need

12-hole muffin tin

large piping bag fitted with a medium star nozzle

1. Preheat the oven to 180°C/350°F/Gas Mark 4. Line a 12-hole muffin tin with paper cases.

2. To make the cupcakes, place all the ingredients (except the food colouring and chocolate chips) in a large bowl and beat with a hand-held electric mixer for 1–2 minutes until smooth and creamy. Beat in enough red food colouring paste to give the mixture a bright red colour.

3. Place a spoonful of the sponge mixture in the base of each paper case, then sprinkle over half the chocolate chips. Spoon over the remaining sponge mixture and scatter over the remaining chocolate chips (see step pic 3).

4. Bake in the preheated oven for 20–25 minutes, or until risen and just firm to the touch. Transfer to a wire rack and leave to cool completely.

5. To decorate, spoon the buttercream into a large piping bag fitted with a medium star nozzle. Pipe stars all over the top of each cupcake to cover completely (see step pic 5).

6. To make the ladybirds, evenly divide the red icing into 12 pieces. Shape each piece into an oval to form the bodies. Shape 12 small pieces of black icing into flat ovals for the faces and attach to the bodies with a dab of the water (see step pic 6). Roll tiny pieces of black icing into dots and attach to the bodies to resemble the ladybirds' spots. Score down the back of each body with a knife to mark the wings. Use the black and white writing icing to dot eyes on the faces.

3

5

6

Tip

You can make the ladybirds a few days in advance. Leave on a board, uncovered, for 3–4 hours until they are dry then store in an airtight container for up to 1 week.

CHEQUERBOARD CAKE

Moist mocha- and orange-flavoured sponges are simply cut into rings and re-assembled to create this stunning chequerboard effect.

Serves 12 >> **Prep time:** 1 hr 15 mins, plus time to cool & chill >> **Cooking time:** 1 hr

Chocolate sponges

2 tbsp cocoa powder

1 tsp instant coffee granules

2 tbsp hot water

225 g/8 oz self-raising flour

225 g/8 oz butter, softened, plus extra for greasing

225 g/8 oz caster sugar

4 eggs

25 g/1 oz ground almonds

2 tbsp milk

Orange sponges

225 g/8 oz self-raising flour

225 g/8 oz butter, softened

225 g/8 oz caster sugar

4 eggs

40 g/1½ oz ground almonds

2 tbsp orange juice

To decorate

1 quantity glossy chocolate frosting (see page 9)

2–3 tbsp white chocolate and plain chocolate mini chips

You will also need

2 x 18-cm/7-inch round sandwich tins

6-cm/2½-inch round metal cutter

12-cm/4½-inch saucer

1. Preheat the oven to 180°C/350°F/Gas Mark 4. Grease 2 x 18-cm/7-inch round sandwich tins and base-line with baking paper.

2. To make the chocolate sponges, mix together the cocoa powder, coffee granules and hot water in a small bowl to make a smooth paste. Set aside. Sift the flour into a large bowl and add the butter, sugar, eggs, ground almonds and milk. Beat with a hand-held electric mixer for 1–2 minutes until smooth and creamy, then beat in the cocoa paste.

3. Divide the mixture evenly between the prepared tins (see step pic 3) and bake in the preheated oven for 30 minutes, or until risen and just firm to the touch. Leave to cool in the tins for 10 minutes, then turn out onto a wire rack and leave to cool completely. Do not switch off the oven. Clean the tins, then grease and base-line with baking paper.

4. To make the orange sponges, sift the flour into a large bowl and add the butter, sugar, eggs and ground almonds. Beat with a hand-held electric mixer for 1–2 minutes until smooth and creamy, then beat in the orange juice.

5. Divide the mixture evenly between the prepared tins and bake in the preheated oven for 25–30 minutes, or until risen and just firm to the touch. Leave to cool in the tins for 10 minutes, then turn out onto a wire rack and leave to cool completely.

P.T.O.

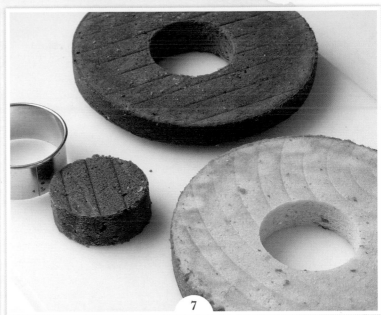

6. Place the cold cakes in the freezer and leave them to chill for about 30 minutes until quite firm. Place the chilled cakes on two large boards. If the tops of the cakes are slightly uneven use a serrated knife to level them.

7. Using a 6-cm/2½-inch round metal cutter, stamp out a round from the centre of each cake and carefully remove (see step pic 7).

8. Then, using a 12-cm/4½-inch saucer as a guide, cut a ring of sponge from each cake. Very carefully separate and remove the rings, leaving 4 outer rings of sponge (see step pic 8).

9. Re-assemble the cakes, swapping the chocolate and orange sponge circles and rings so you end up with 4 sponge cakes that look like targets (see step pic 9). Handle the rings very carefully to prevent cracking.

10. To decorate, spread a thin layer of frosting over one of the sponge cakes and top with a second alternate sponge cake (see step pic 10). Repeat to stack up all the layers neatly, making sure you alternate the sponges as you go to ensure a chequerboard appearance when you cut into the cake.

11. Spread the remaining frosting in an even layer around the sides and over the top of the cake, smoothing it with a palette knife (see step pic 11). Decorate the top and around the bottom edges of the cake with mini chocolate chips.

Tip

Don't chill the cakes in the freezer for too long or they may crack when you cut them into rings. If they have become too firm, leave at room temperature for 5–10 minutes.

RED VELVET CHEESECAKE CAKE

This indulgent cake makes an ideal party dessert with a rich and creamy layer of baked vanilla cheesecake sandwiched between two classic red velvet sponge cakes.

Serves 12 >> **Prep time:** 1 hr, plus time to cool & chill >> **Cooking time:** 1 hr 5 mins

Cheesecake

400 g/14 oz full-fat soft cheese

85 g/3 oz caster sugar

1 tsp vanilla extract

2 eggs, beaten

100 ml/3½ fl oz soured cream

1 tbsp cornflour

Red velvet cakes

200 g/7 oz plain flour

1½ tsp bicarbonate of soda

3 tbsp cocoa powder

175 g/6 oz butter, softened, plus extra for greasing

200 g/7 oz caster sugar

2 eggs, beaten

150 ml/5 fl oz buttermilk

1 tsp vanilla extract

2 tbsp red liquid food colouring

To decorate

1 quantity cream cheese frosting (see page 10)

40 g/1½ oz plain chocolate, melted

You will also need

18-cm/7-inch round springform tin

2 x 18-cm/7-inch round sandwich tins

small paper piping bag

1. Preheat the oven to 160°C/325°F/Gas Mark 3. Grease an 18-cm/7-inch round springform tin and base-line with baking paper. Wrap a layer of foil around the base and up the sides of the tin and place it on a baking sheet.

2. To make the cheesecake, place the cheese, sugar and vanilla extract in a large bowl and beat together until smooth. Gradually beat in the eggs, then add the soured cream and cornflour, stirring until smooth.

3. Spoon the mixture into the prepared tin and gently level the surface. Bake in the preheated oven for 35 minutes, or until just set but still slightly wobbly in the centre. Switch off the oven and leave the cheesecake to cool in the oven with the door ajar. When it has cooled completely, cover the top of the tin with a sheet of baking paper and place it in the refrigerator for at least 4 hours or overnight.

4. To make the red velvet cakes, preheat the oven to 180°C/350°F/Gas Mark 4. Grease 2 x 18-cm/7-inch round sandwich tins and base-line with baking paper. Sift together the flour, bicarbonate of soda and cocoa powder into a bowl and set aside.

5. Place the butter and sugar in a large bowl and beat together with a hand-held electric mixer until pale and fluffy. Gradually beat in the eggs, then beat in the buttermilk, vanilla extract and food colouring. Fold in the sifted flour mixture (see step pic 5).

P.T.O.

6. Divide the mixture evenly between the prepared tins and level the surfaces. Bake in the preheated oven for 30 minutes, or until risen and just firm to the touch. Leave to cool in the tins for 10 minutes, then turn out onto a wire rack and leave to cool completely.

7. Unclip and remove the springform sides from the cheesecake. Place one red velvet cake on top of the cheesecake (see step pic 7).

8. Invert the cake and cheesecake onto a board or serving plate and carefully remove the base of the tin and the lining paper. Gently place the second cake on top (see step pic 8).

9. Spread a thin layer of the frosting around the sides and over the top of the layered cake. Place in the refrigerator for 30 minutes.

10. Spread the remaining frosting all over the cake, smoothing it lightly with a palette knife (see step pic 10). Spoon the melted chocolate into a small paper piping bag. Snip off the end and pipe swirls on top of the cake. Chill in the refrigerator until ready to serve.

Tip

To melt chocolate, break the chocolate into pieces and place in a large heatproof bowl. Set the bowl over a pan of simmering water, making sure the bowl does not touch the water, and leave until the chocolate has melted. Remove the bowl from the pan and stir the chocolate until smooth.

POPPING CANDY CUPCAKES

These cupcakes will certainly set the taste buds tingling with a secret surprise of cracking popping candy tucked away inside.

Makes 12 >> **Prep time:** 20 mins, plus time to cool >> **Cooking time:** 15–20 mins

115 g/4 oz self-raising flour

¼ tsp baking powder

115 g/4 oz butter, softened

115 g/4 oz caster sugar

2 large eggs, beaten

½ tsp vanilla extract

1 tbsp milk

pink food colouring paste or gel

40 g/1½ oz popping candy

To decorate

1 quantity pink buttercream
(see page 8)

pink shimmer sugar sprinkles

You will also need

12-hole muffin tin

large piping bag fitted with a large star nozzle

1. Preheat the oven to 180°C/350°F/Gas Mark 4. Line a 12-hole muffin tin with paper cases.

2. Sift together the flour and baking powder into a large bowl. Add the butter, sugar, eggs, vanilla extract and milk. Beat with a hand-held electric mixer for 1–2 minutes until smooth and creamy. Beat in enough food colouring to give the mixture a mid-pink colour (see step pic 2).

3. Divide the mixture evenly between the paper cases (see step pic 3). Bake in the preheated oven for 15–20 minutes, or until risen, golden and firm to the touch. Transfer to a wire rack and leave to cool.

4. Use a small serrated knife to cut a cone shape out of the centre of each cupcake. Place about 1 teaspoon of popping candy into each hollow. Slice off the tip of each cone shape, then replace the cones on top of the popping candy to cover completely (see step pic 4).

5. To decorate, spoon the buttercream into a large piping bag fitted with a large star nozzle. Pipe swirls of frosting on top of each cupcake and sprinkle with pink shimmer sugar sprinkles.

Tip
You can make the cupcakes a day in advance or freeze them for up to two months, but only fill and frost just before serving or the candy will lose its 'pop'.

PINK OMBRE CAKE

With both sponge and frosting delicately shaded from dark to light pink this cake has a very sophisticated look. You can vary the colour theme as you please, shades of purple, blue, orange or yellow will all work well.

Serves 10 >> **Prep time:** 1 hr, plus time to cool & chill >> **Cooking time:** 15–18 mins

225 g/8 oz self-raising flour

½ tsp baking powder

225 g/8 oz butter, softened, plus extra for greasing

225 g/8 oz caster sugar

4 large eggs

2 tbsp milk

2 tsp rosewater

pink food colouring paste or gel

To decorate
1½ quantity buttercream (see page 8)

pink food colouring paste or gel

1 tbsp edible shimmer pearls

You will also need
4 x 18-cm/7-inch round sandwich tins

1. Preheat the oven to 180°C/350°F/Gas Mark 4. Grease 4 x 18-cm/7-inch round sandwich tins and base-line with baking paper.

2. Sift together the flour and baking powder into a large mixing bowl and add the butter, sugar, eggs, milk and rosewater. Beat with a hand-held electric mixer for 1–2 minutes until pale and creamy (see step pic 2). Weigh the mixture, then divide it equally between four bowls.

3. Beat increasing amounts of pink food colouring paste into each of the bowls of mixture to give four distinctly different shades of pink from pale to very bright (see step pic 3). Spoon each bowl of mixture into a prepared tin and gently level the surface.

4. Bake in the preheated oven for 15–18 minutes, or until risen and just firm to the touch. Leave to cool in the tins for 5 minutes, then turn out onto two wire racks and leave to cool completely.

5. To decorate, use a quarter of the buttercream to sandwich the 4 layers of sponge together. Start with the darkest pink sponge at the bottom and finish with the lightest pink sponge on top (see step pic 5). Spread a thin layer of the buttercream around the sides and over the top of the cake and chill in the refrigerator for 30 minutes.

6. Place half of the remaining buttercream in a smaller bowl and add enough pink colouring paste to give a pale pink colour. Divide the remaining buttercream between two small bowls and colour one half mid-pink and the other half bright pink (see step pic 6).

P.T.O.

7. Using a palette knife, spread the bright pink buttercream around the sides of the bottom third of the assembled cake. Spread the mid-pink buttercream around the middle of the cake, merging it a little with the bright pink buttercream (see step pic 7).

8. Spread the pale pink buttercream around the sides of the top of the cake, merging it a little with the mid-pink buttercream. Spread the remaining pale pink buttercream over the top of the cake, swirling it with the palette knife (see step pic 8). Scatter the shimmer pearls over the top just before serving.

Tip

If you only have two tins, make the cakes in two batches, but reserve a little of the coloured mixtures from the first batch so you can match the shading.

HIDDEN HEARTS SPONGE CAKE

Slice into this classic almond-flavoured Victoria sponge cake to discover tiny marzipan hearts. It's the perfect way to say 'I love you' to someone special.

Serves 8 >> **Prep time:** 45 mins, plus time to cool >> **Cooking time:** 25–30 mins

225 g/8 oz butter, softened, plus extra for greasing

225 g/8 oz caster sugar

4 large eggs, beaten

225 g/8 oz self-raising flour

1 tsp almond extract

1 tbsp milk

To decorate

icing sugar, for dusting

225 g/8 oz natural marzipan

red food colouring paste

1 quantity buttercream, (see page 8)

You will also need

2 x 20-cm/8-inch round sandwich tins

thin metal skewer

small heart-shaped cutter

1. Preheat the oven to 180°C/350°F/Gas Mark 4. Grease 2 x 20-cm/8-inch round sandwich tins and base-line with baking paper.

2. Place the butter and sugar in a bowl and beat together until pale and creamy. Gradually beat in the eggs, adding a spoonful of the flour if the mixture starts to curdle. Sift in the flour and gently fold in using a metal spoon. Fold in the almond extract and milk.

3. Divide the mixture evenly between the prepared tins and level the surfaces. Bake in the preheated oven for 25–30 minutes, or until risen, golden and just firm to the touch. Leave to cool in the tins for 10 minutes, then turn out onto a wire rack and leave to cool completely.

4. To decorate, lightly dust a surface with icing sugar, then knead the marzipan until smooth. Knead in enough food colouring paste to colour the marzipan bright red.

5. Take a 70-g/2½-oz piece of marzipan and thinly roll out to a 35-cm/14-inch long roll. Then take a 50-g/1¾-oz piece of marzipan and roll to a 20-cm/8-inch long roll (see step pic 5).

6. Form the rolls into heart shapes by first scoring along the length of each roll with a knife. Run a thin metal skewer along the scored lines to shape the top of the heart. Turn the rolls over and pinch along the length of each roll to shape the pointed base of the heart (see step pic 6).

5

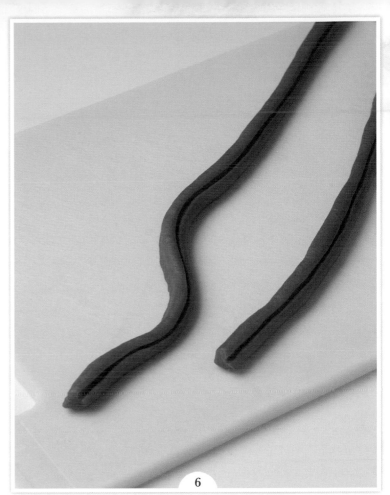

6

7

8

7. Spread one third of the buttercream on one of the sponges. Arrange the heart-shaped rolls, point side down, in two concentric circles on the buttercream, pressing them down gently (see step pic 7). Spread another third of the buttercream over the marzipan rolls in an even layer. Place the second sponge on top.

8. Spread the remaining buttercream over the top sponge, swirling it into circles with the tip of a palette knife. Thinly roll out the remaining marzipan on a surface lightly dusted with icing sugar. Use a small heart-shaped cutter to stamp out 8 marzipan hearts and arrange them on the top of the cake (see step pic 8).

Tip

To colour the marzipan, dip a cocktail stick into the food colouring paste and transfer it to the marzipan. Knead in and repeat until you have the depth of colour you require.

COOKIES & CREAM CUPCAKES

These moreish cupcakes are packed with crushed chocolate cookies and have a lovely crisp cookie base too. Topped with swirls of tangy cream cheese frosting they won't be around for long!

Makes 12 >> **Prep time:** 20 mins, plus time to cool >> **Cooking time:** 20–25 mins

20 round chocolate sandwich cookies

115 g/4 oz butter, softened

115 g/4 oz caster sugar

2 large eggs, beaten

115 g/4 oz self-raising flour

½ tsp vanilla extract

1 tbsp milk

To decorate

2 quantities cream cheese frosting, chilled (see page 10)

14 round mini chocolate sandwich cookies

You will also need

12-hole muffin tin

large piping bag fitted with a large star nozzle

1. Preheat the oven to 180°C/350°F/Gas Mark 4. Line a 12-hole muffin tin with paper cases and place a cookie in the base of each case (see step pic 1). Roughly chop the remaining cookies and set aside.

2. Place the butter and sugar in a bowl and beat until pale and creamy. Gradually beat in the eggs, adding a spoonful of the flour if the mixture starts to curdle. Sift in the flour and fold in gently using a metal spoon. Fold in the vanilla extract, milk and chopped cookies.

3. Divide the mixture evenly between the paper cases (see step pic 3) Bake in the preheated oven for 20–25 minutes, or until risen, golden and firm to the touch. Transfer to a wire rack and leave to cool.

4. To decorate, spoon the frosting into a large piping bag fitted with a large star nozzle. Pipe swirls of frosting on top of each cupcake and top each with a mini cookie (see step pic 4).

5. Halve the remaining mini cookies, discard the cream filling, then finely crush the cookies and sprinkle the crumbs over the frosting.

Tip

Don't chop the cookies too finely; you want to have nice big chunks in the mixture.

BABY BOY OR GIRL CAKE

This is a fun, edible way to reveal whether you are expecting a new baby boy or girl – just fill the centre of the cake with pink or blue sweets.

 Serves 8 >> **Prep time:** 1 hr, plus time to cool >> **Cooking time:** 25–30 mins

225 g/8 oz self-raising flour

½ tsp baking powder

225 g/8 oz butter, plus extra for greasing

225 g/8 oz caster sugar

4 eggs

1 tsp vanilla extract

To decorate

⅓ quantity buttercream (see page 8)

175 g/6 oz pink or blue sweets, such as sugar-coated chocolate drops or sugared almonds

500 g/1 lb 2 oz white ready-to-roll icing

icing sugar, for dusting

baby blue and pink food colouring paste or gel

You will also need

3 x 15-cm/6-inch round sandwich tins

7-cm/2¾-inch round metal cutter

small round cutter

small paintbrush

1. Preheat the oven to 180°C/350°F/Gas Mark 4. Grease 3 x 15-cm/6-inch round sandwich tins and base-line with baking paper.

2. Sift together the flour and baking powder into a large bowl. Add the butter, sugar, eggs and vanilla extract and beat with a hand-held electric mixer for 1–2 minutes until smooth and creamy. Weigh the mixture and divide equally between the prepared tins. Gently level the surfaces.

3. Bake in the preheated oven for 25–30 minutes, or until risen and just firm to the touch. Leave to cool in the tins for 10 minutes, then turn out onto a wire rack and leave to cool completely.

4. To assemble, use a 7-cm/2¾-inch round metal cutter to stamp out a round from the centre of one of the cakes to make a ring. Press the cutter into the centre of the other two cakes to a depth of about 1 cm/½ inch and scoop out some of the sponge to make a dip in the centre of each cake (see step pic 4).

5. Place one of the whole cakes (dip side up) on a board and spread a quarter of the buttercream all around the rim of the dip. Place the ring cake on top. Spread another quarter of the buttercream over this cake.

6. Fill the hollow with pink or blue sweets (see step pic 6). Place the second whole sponge on top (dip side down). Spread the remaining buttercream in a thin layer around the sides and over the top of the cake.

P.T.O.

4

6

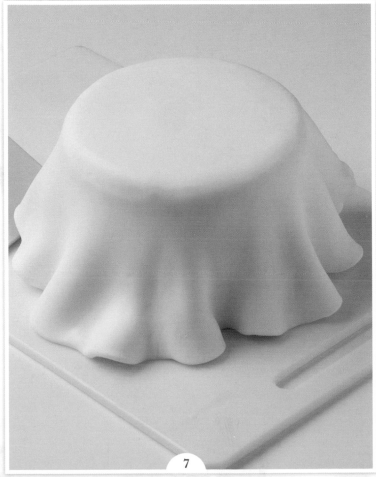

7

9

7. Roll out the icing on a surface lightly dusted with icing sugar to a 35-cm/14-inch round. Gently lift the icing onto a rolling pin and drape it over the cake, allowing it to fall down the sides (see step pic 7). Gently smooth out any folds and creases with your hands. Trim off the excess icing with a small knife.

8. Re-knead the icing trimmings until smooth and divide in two. Use the blue and pink colouring paste to colour one half of the icing baby blue and the other half pale pink.

9. Thinly roll out each piece of icing on a surface lightly dusted with icing sugar and use a small round cutter to stamp out small rounds – about 15 of each colour. Attach the circles to the cake in a random design with a dampened paintbrush (see step pic 9).

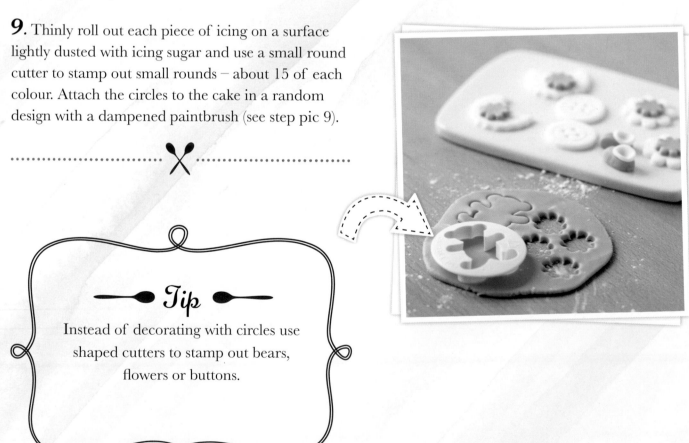

Tip

Instead of decorating with circles use shaped cutters to stamp out bears, flowers or buttons.

POLKA DOT CAKE

Amaze your guests with this incredible chocolate cake studded inside with vibrant blue sponge polka dots. Much easier to make than you may think, you just need to invest in a cake pop mould.

Serves 10 >> **Prep time:** 1 hr 30 mins, plus time to cool >> **Cooking time:** 1 hr

Blue sponge balls

100 g/3½ oz self-raising flour, sifted

100 g/3½ oz butter, softened, plus extra for greasing

100 g/3½ oz caster sugar

2 eggs

blue food colouring paste or gel

Chocolate sponges

200 g/7 oz self-raising flour

35 g/1¼ oz cocoa powder

225 g/8 oz butter, softened, plus extra for greasing

225 g/8 oz caster sugar

4 large eggs

4 tbsp milk

To decorate

1 quantity glossy chocolate frosting (see page 9)

blue sugar-coated chocolate drops

You will also need

20-hole silicone cake pop mould

2 x 17-cm/6½-inch round silicone cake moulds

---

1. Preheat the oven to 180°C/350°F/Gas Mark 4. Lightly grease both halves of a 20-hole silicone cake pop mould and place the bottom mould on a baking sheet.

2. To make the blue sponge balls, place the flour, butter, sugar and eggs in a large bowl and beat with a hand-held electric mixer for 1–2 minutes until smooth and creamy. Beat in enough of the food colouring paste to give the mixture a bright blue colour (see step pic 2).

3. Use a teaspoon to distribute the mixture evenly in the bottom mould, taking care not to overfill each dip in the cake mould (see step pic 3). Then place the other mould on top. Bake in the preheated oven for 20 minutes, or until the sponge balls are risen and firm to the touch. Leave the cakes in the moulds for 20 minutes, then carefully remove them, trimming off any excess sponge around the balls with the tip of a small knife. Transfer to a wire rack and leave to cool completely. Do not switch off the oven.

4. To make the chocolate sponges, sift together the flour and cocoa powder into a large bowl and add the butter, sugar and eggs. Beat with a hand-held electric mixer for 1–2 minutes until smooth and creamy, then beat in the milk (see step pic 4).

5. Grease 2 x 17-cm/6½-inch round silicone cake moulds and place on a large baking sheet. Divide the chocolate sponge mixture in two. Spread one third of each quantity in the base of each silicone mould. Arrange 10 sponge balls in each mould, placing 1 in the centre and the remaining 9 in a circle (see step pic 5).

P.T.O.

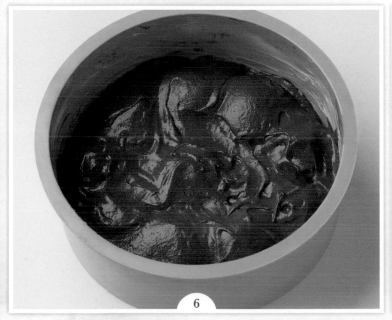

POLKA DOT
CAKE CONTINUED...

6. Spoon the remainder of each mixture into each cake mould, making sure the mixture goes down around the sides of the sponge balls. Gently level the surface with a palette knife (see step pic 6).

7. Bake in the preheated oven for 35–40 minutes, or until the cakes are risen and just firm to the touch. Leave to cool in the moulds for 10 minutes, then carefully turn out onto a wire rack and leave to cool completely.

8. To decorate, sandwich the two sponges together with a quarter of the frosting. Spread the remaining frosting around the sides and over the top of the cake, smoothing and swirling it with a palette knife (see step pic 8). Gently press the sugar-coated chocolate drops around the edge of the top of the cake.

Tip

Try using a different colour for the cake balls inside, or divide the cake mixture between bowls and use 3 or 4 different colours for a rainbow effect.

NEAPOLITAN CAKE

This colourful cake will make a stunning centrepiece for a summer afternoon tea with layers of chocolate, strawberry and vanilla sponge covered in swirls of pink and white frosting.

Serves 10 >> **Prep time:** 1 hr, plus time to cool & chill >> **Cooking time:** 25–30 mins

1½ tbsp cocoa powder, sifted

1½ tbsp hot water

225 g/8 oz self-raising flour

½ tsp baking powder

225 g/8 oz butter, softened, plus extra for greasing

225 g/8 oz caster sugar

4 eggs

2 tbsp milk

½ tsp vanilla extract

½ tsp strawberry extract

pink food colouring paste or gel

To decorate

1½ quantities buttercream (see page 8)

pink food colouring paste or gel

You will also need

3 x 15-cm/6-inch round sandwich tins

large piping bag fitted with a medium star nozzle

1. Preheat the oven to 180°C/350°F/Gas Mark 4. Grease 3 x 15-cm/6-inch round sandwich tins and base-line with baking paper. Mix together the cocoa powder and hot water in a small bowl to make a smooth paste and set aside.

2. Sift together the flour and baking powder into a large bowl and add the butter, sugar, eggs and milk. Beat with a hand-held electric mixer for 1–2 minutes until smooth and creamy (see step pic 2). Weigh the mixture and divide equally into three separate bowls.

3. Beat the chocolate paste into one bowl of mixture. Beat the vanilla extract into the second bowl of mixture. Beat the strawberry extract and enough food colouring to give a bright pink colour into the third bowl of mixture.

4. Spoon the mixtures into the prepared tins and gently level the surfaces. Bake in the preheated oven for 25 minutes, or until risen and just firm to the touch. The chocolate sponge may need an extra 4–5 minutes. Leave to cool in the tins for 10 minutes, then turn out onto a wire rack and leave to cool completely (see step pic 4).

5. To decorate, use some of the buttercream to sandwich the three sponges together, with the chocolate sponge at the bottom and the vanilla sponge at the top (see step pic 5). Spread a thin layer of buttercream around the sides and over the top of the stacked cakes. Place in the refrigerator for 30 minutes.

P.T.O.

6. Divide the remaining buttercream between two bowls. Use the pink food colouring to colour one bowl of buttercream deep pink. Use a spatula to spoon the pink buttercream down one side of a large piping bag fitted with a medium star nozzle. Spoon the white buttercream down the other side of the piping bag.

7. Starting at the base, pipe three rosettes of buttercream up the side of the cake. Repeat all around the cake until the sides are completely covered (see step pic 7). Pipe rosettes in concentric circles over the top of the cake.

Tip

For a simpler decoration, use a half quantity of buttercream to sandwich and cover the cakes, spreading the buttercream smooth with a palette knife. Press rows of pink, white and milk chocolate buttons onto the sides and top of the cake.

HALLOWEEN BAT CAKE

This is the ideal cake to make for a spooky Halloween party. The scary surprise inside this cake will keep trick or treaters guessing all evening!

Serves 8 >> **Prep time:** 1 hr 10 mins, plus time to cool & chill >> **Cooking time:** 1 hr 25 mins–1 hr 45 mins

Black sponge

115 g/4 oz self-raising flour

¼ tsp baking powder

115 g/4 oz butter, softened, plus extra for greasing

115 g/4 oz caster sugar

2 large eggs

1 tbsp black food colouring paste or gel

Spiced sponge

200 g/7 oz self-raising flour

175 g/6 oz butter, softened, plus extra for greasing

100 g/3½ oz caster sugar

70 g/2½ oz light muscovado sugar

3 eggs

2 tbsp maple syrup

1 tsp mixed spice

To decorate

1 quantity cream cheese frosting (see page 10)

You will also need

900-g/2-lb loaf tin

bat-shaped cookie cutter

1. Preheat the oven to 180°C/350°F/Gas Mark 4. Grease a 900-g/2-lb loaf tin and line the base and two long sides with baking paper.

2. To make the black sponge, place the flour, baking powder, butter, sugar and eggs in a large bowl and beat with a hand-held electric mixer for 1–2 minutes until smooth and creamy. Beat in the black food colouring.

3. Spoon the mixture into the prepared tin and level the surface. Bake in the preheated oven for 30–40 minutes, or until risen, firm to the touch and a skewer inserted into the middle of the cake comes out clean. Leave to cool in the tin for 10 minutes, then turn out onto a wire rack and leave to cool completely. Switch off the oven. Clean the tin, then grease and line the base and two long sides with baking paper.

4. When the cake is completely cold use a sharp knife to cut it into 10 even-sized slices (see step pic 4). Arrange cut-side down on a board and place in the freezer for about 25 minutes.

5. Meanwhile, preheat the oven to 160°C/325°F/Gas Mark 3.

6. To make the spiced sponge, place all the ingredients in a large bowl and beat together with a hand-held electric mixer for 1–2 minutes until smooth and creamy. Spoon about half the mixture into the prepared tin and use a palette knife to angle the mixture up one side of the tin (see step pic 6).

P.T.O.

7. Use a bat-shaped cookie cutter to stamp out 10 bat shapes from the chilled black sponge slices (see step pic 7).

8. Arrange the bat shapes along the length of mixture in the cake tin, making sure the slices line up at the same angle and are as close together as possible (see step pic 8).

9. Spoon the remaining spiced sponge mixture into the tin, spooning it around and over the bat shapes to cover them completely (see step pic 9). Gently level the surface.

10. Bake in the preheated oven for 55 minutes–1 hour 5 minutes, or until the sponge is risen and golden and a skewer inserted into the middle of the cake comes out clean. Leave to cool in the tin for 15 minutes, then transfer to a wire rack and leave to cool completely.

11. To decorate, use a palette knife to spread the cream cheese frosting over the top of the cold cake (see step pic 11).

Tip

If you want to decorate your cake with a Halloween theme, make simple pumpkin decorations with orange fondant icing and green jelly sweets.

TUMBLING BERRIES GATEAU

This cake is a delicious variation on a classic summer fruit gateau with sweet juicy berries hidden inside just ready to come tumbling out. Serve with extra berries or a fresh fruit coulis for a special dessert.

Serves 12 >> **Prep time:** 45 mins, plus time to cool & chill >> **Cooking time:** 25–30 mins

350 g/12 oz butter, softened, plus extra for greasing

350 g/12 oz caster sugar

6 eggs, beaten

350 g/12 oz self-raising flour

1 tsp vanilla extract

2 tbsp milk

Filling & decoration

1 quantity mascarpone cream frosting (see page 10)

300 g/10½ oz mixed summer berries, such as raspberries, redcurrants, blueberries and small strawberries

You will also need

3 x 20-cm/8-inch round sandwich tins

14-cm/5½-inch saucer

1. Preheat the oven to 180°C/350°F/Gas Mark 4. Grease 3 x 20-cm/8-inch round sandwich tins and base-line with baking paper.

2. Place the butter and sugar in a bowl and beat together until pale and creamy. Gradually beat in the eggs, adding a spoonful of the flour if the mixture starts to curdle. Sift in the flour and gently fold in with a metal spoon. Fold in the vanilla extract and milk.

3. Divide the mixture between the prepared tins and gently level the surfaces. Bake in the preheated oven for 25–30 minutes, or until risen and just firm to the touch. Leave to cool in the tins for 10 minutes, then turn out onto a wire rack and leave to cool completely.

4. To fill and decorate the cake, cut out the centre of one of the sponge cakes, using a 14-cm/5½-inch saucer as a guide, to make a ring. Place one whole cake on a board and spread some of the frosting around the cake in a 3-cm/1¼-inch border. Place the cake with the centre removed on top (see step pic 4).

5. Fill the centre of the middle cake with two thirds of the berries (see step pic 5). Spread some more of the frosting around the rim of the middle cake. Gently place the second whole cake on top.

6. Spread some of the remaining frosting in a thin layer around the sides of the cake. Chill the cake in the refrigerator for 15 minutes.

7. Spread two thirds of the remaining frosting around the sides of the cake, smoothing it into vertical lines with the tip of a small palette knife (see step pic 7). Spread the remaining frosting over the top of the cake and decorate with the remaining berries.

4

5

7

Tip

The sponges can be made a day in advance or frozen for up to 2 months but only assemble and decorate the cake a few hours before serving or the juice from the fruit will seep into the sponges.

TROPICAL SUNRISE CAKE

Be prepared for gasps of wonder when you slice into this cake. It's a real work of art yet surprisingly easy to create when you know the secret technique!

Serves **10** >> *Prep time:* 1 hr 15 mins, plus time to cool & chill >> *Cooking time:* 2 hrs 5 mins–2 hrs 15 mins

Chocolate sponge

150 g/5½ oz self-raising flour

½ tsp baking powder

25 g/1 oz cocoa powder

175 g/6 oz butter, softened, plus extra for greasing

175 g/6 oz caster sugar

3 large eggs

Sunset sponge

200 g/7 oz self-raising flour

175 g/6 oz butter, softened

175 g/6 oz caster sugar

3 large eggs

2 tbsp milk

red, orange and yellow food colouring pastes or gel

To decorate

½ quantity glossy chocolate frosting (see page 9)

You will also need

900-g/2-lb loaf tin measuring 20 cm/8 inches long and at least 8 cm/3¼ inches deep

palm tree-shaped cookie cutter

1. Preheat the oven to 180°C/350°F/Gas Mark 4. Grease a 900-g/2-lb loaf tin measuring 20 cm/8 inches long and at least 8 cm/3¼ inches deep. Line the base and two long sides with baking paper.

2. To make the chocolate sponge, sift together the flour, baking powder and cocoa powder into a large bowl and add the butter, sugar and eggs. Beat with a hand-held electric mixer for 1–2 minutes until smooth and creamy.

3. Spoon the mixture into the prepared tin and level the surface. Bake in the preheated oven for 45–50 minutes, or until risen, firm to the touch and a skewer inserted into the middle of the cake comes out clean. Leave to cool in the tin for 10 minutes, then turn out onto a wire rack and leave to cool completely. Turn off the oven.

4. When the cake has cooled completely use a sharp knife to cut it into 8 even-sized slices. Arrange cut-side down on a board and place in the freezer for 30 minutes. When the slices are firm, use a palm tree-shaped cookie cutter to stamp out 8 chocolate sponge palm trees (see step pic 4). Return to the freezer for a further 20–30 minutes, or until firm.

5. Meanwhile, preheat the oven to 160°C/325°F/Gas Mark 3. Clean and grease the loaf tin and line the base and two long sides with baking paper.

P.T.O.

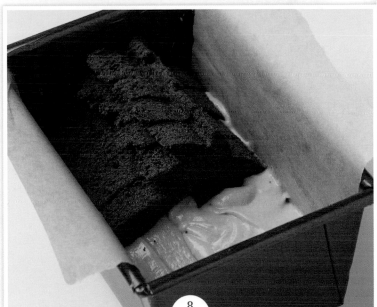

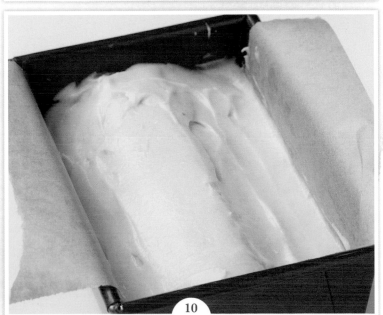

6. To make the sunset sponge, place all the ingredients (except the food colourings) in a large bowl and beat with a hand-held electric mixer for 1–2 minutes until smooth and creamy. Divide the mixture into 3 bowls of roughly equal quantities. Use the colouring pastes to colour one bowl of mixture pale red, one orange and one yellow (see step pic 6).

7. Spoon the pale red mixture into the base of the prepared tin in an even layer. Spoon just over half the orange mixture along the length of half the tin (see step pic 7).

8. Arrange the chilled chocolate palm trees along the length of the mixture in the tin, making sure the slices line up at the same angle and are as close together as possible (see step pic 8).

9. When all the palm trees are in the tin spoon the remaining orange mixture over the tree trunks (see step pic 9).

10. Spoon the yellow mixture over the palm trees to cover them completely. Use a small angled palette knife to gently spread the mixture, taking care not to knock the palm trees (see step pic 10).

11. Bake in the preheated oven for 1 hour 20 minutes–1 hour 25 minutes, or until the sponge is risen and golden and a skewer inserted into the middle of the cake comes out clean. Loosely cover the top with foil after 1 hour 10 minutes if the top of the cake is becoming too brown. Leave to cool in the tin for 15 minutes, then turn out onto a wire rack and leave to cool completely.

12. To decorate, use a palette knife to spread the glossy chocolate frosting in a thick layer over the top of the cold cake.

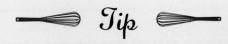

Tip

Try and place the palm trees as close together as possible to stop the sponge mixture bubbling up through them when the cake is baked.

CHRISTMAS TREE WREATH CAKE

Celebrate the festive season with this delightful themed cake with the added surprise of Christmas tree sponge running through the middle.

Serves 16 >> **Prep time:** 1 hr, plus time to cool & chill >> **Cooking time:** 1 hr 45 mins–1 hr 55 mins

Green sponge

225 g/8 oz self-raising flour, plus extra for dusting

¼ tsp baking powder

225 g/8 oz butter, softened, plus extra for greasing

225 g/8 oz caster sugar

4 large eggs

green food colouring paste or gel

Vanilla sponge

250 g/9 oz self-raising flour

225 g/8 oz butter, softened

225 g/8 oz caster sugar

4 large eggs

1 tsp vanilla extract

To decorate

1 quantity buttercream (see page 8)

2 tsp red, white and green confetti sugar sprinkles

1 tsp edible silver balls (optional)

You will also need

2-litre/3½-pint ring cake tin (at least 8 cm/3¼ inches deep)

7 cm/2¾ inch tall Christmas tree-shaped cookie cutter

large disposable piping bag fitted with a medium plain nozzle

1. Preheat the oven to 160°C/325°F/Gas Mark 3. Thoroughly grease a 2-litre/3½-pint ring cake tin (at least 8 cm/3¼ inches deep), then lightly dust with flour.

2. To make the green sponge, place the flour, baking powder, butter, sugar and eggs in a large bowl and beat with a hand-held electric mixer for 1–2 minutes until smooth and creamy. Beat in enough green food colouring paste to give the mixture a Christmas tree-green colour.

3. Spoon the mixture into the prepared tin and level the surface. Bake in the preheated oven for 45–50 minutes, or until risen, firm to the touch and a skewer inserted into the middle of the cake comes out clean. Leave to cool in the tin for 10 minutes, then turn out carefully onto a wire rack and leave to cool completely. Switch off the oven.

4. When the cake is completely cold, place it on a board and use a sharp knife to cut it into 16 wedge-shaped slices (see step 4). Slightly separate the slices (still maintaining the ring shape), then place in the freezer for 30 minutes.

5. Use a 7 cm/2¾ inch tall Christmas tree-shaped cookie cutter to stamp out 16 Christmas tree shapes from the chilled sponge wedges. Re-form the trees into the ring shape again (see step pic 5) and return to the freezer for a further 30–40 minutes, or until very firm.

P.T.O.

4

5

8

9

10

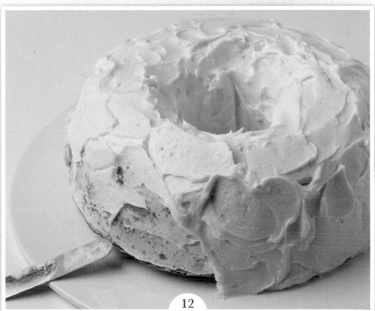

12

6. Meanwhile, preheat the oven to 160°C/325°F/ Gas Mark 3. Clean the tin, thoroughly grease and lightly dust with flour.

7. To make the vanilla sponge, place all the ingredients in a large bowl and beat with a hand-held electric mixer for 1–2 minutes until smooth and creamy. Spoon the mixture into a large disposable piping bag fitted with a medium-sized plain nozzle.

8. Pipe 3 lines of mixture into the base of the prepared tin, then continue piping the mixture up the sides of the centre of tin and smooth with a palette knife (see step pic 8).

9. Take 2 Christmas tree cake shapes together and gently place in the vanilla mixture, pointed side down and leaning into the centre of the tin. Repeat with the remaining slices, keeping them as close together as possible, to re-form the ring shape (upside down) inside the tin (see step pic 9).

10. Pipe the remaining vanilla mixture around the other sides of the trees and over the tops to cover them completely (see step pic 10). Gently level the surface.

11. Bake in the preheated oven for 45 minutes, then loosely cover the top of the cake with foil. Bake for a further 15–20 minutes, or until a skewer inserted into the cake comes out clean (make sure to place the skewer right into the cake in an area where there is more vanilla sponge). Leave to cool in the tin for 15 minutes. Run a small angled palette knife around the sides of the cake, carefully turn out onto a wire rack and leave to cool completely.

12. To decorate, spread some of the buttercream in a thin layer all over the cake. Chill the cake in the refrigerator for 30 minutes. Spread the remaining buttercream all over the cake, swirling it with a palette knife (see step pic 12). Decorate the top of the cake with confetti sprinkles and edible silver balls, if using.

Tip

Once you have the technique perfected why not try a different hidden shape such as a star or gingerbread man? Just make sure the cutter is small enough to fit inside the cake tin.

HIDDEN HEARTS CUPCAKES

These lovely chocolate cupcakes have a pink sponge heart nestling inside them. Perfect to give as a Valentine's Day treat wrapped in a cupcake gift box.

Makes 12 >> **Prep time:** 40 mins, plus time to cool & chill >> **Cooking time:** 40–45 mins

Pink sponge

100 g/3½ oz self-raising flour

¼ tsp baking powder

100 g/3½ oz butter, softened, plus extra for greasing

100 g/3½ oz caster sugar

2 eggs

pink food colouring paste or gel

Chocolate sponge

150 g/5½ oz self-raising flour

25 g/1 oz cocoa powder

¼ tsp baking powder

175 g/6 oz butter, softened

175 g/6 oz caster sugar

3 eggs

1 tbsp milk

To decorate

1 quantity buttercream (see page 8)

1 tbsp heart-shaped red or pink sugar sprinkles

You will also need

18-cm/7-inch round sandwich tin

4-cm/1½-inch wide heart-shaped cutter

12-hole muffin tin

large disposable piping bag fitted with a large plain nozzle

1. Preheat the oven to 180°C/350°F/Gas Mark 4. Grease an 18-cm/7-inch round sandwich tin and base-line with baking paper.

2. To make the pink sponge, place the flour, baking powder, butter, sugar and eggs in a large bowl and beat with a hand-held electric mixer for 1–2 minutes until smooth and creamy. Beat in enough of the pink food colouring to colour the mixture deep pink (see step pic 2).

3. Spoon the mixture into the prepared tin and level the surface. Bake in the preheated oven for 20–25 minutes, or until risen and just firm to the touch. Leave to cool in the tin for 10 minutes, then turn out onto a wire rack and leave to cool completely. Turn off the oven.

4. When the cake has cooled completely, transfer it to a board and place it in the freezer for about 30 minutes.

5. Use a 4-cm/1½-inch wide heart-shaped cutter to stamp out 12 heart shapes from the chilled cake (see step pic 5). Return the hearts to the freezer and freeze for a further 30 minutes. Meanwhile, preheat the oven to 180°C/350°F/Gas Mark 4. Line a 12-hole muffin tin with paper cases.

6. To make the chocolate sponge, place all the ingredients in a large bowl and beat with a hand-held electric mixer for 1–2 minutes until smooth and creamy.

P.T.O.

7. Place a spoonful of chocolate sponge mixture in the base of each paper case, then gently place a chilled pink sponge heart upright on the mixture (see step pic 7).

8. Spoon the remaining chocolate sponge mixture into a large disposable piping bag fitted with a large plain nozzle. Pipe the mixture around the hearts and use the tip of a palette knife to spread the mixture to cover the top of the hearts as much as possible (see step pic 8).

9. Bake in the preheated oven for 20 minutes, or until risen and just firm to the touch. Transfer to a wire rack and leave to cool completely.

10. To decorate, use a palette knife to swirl the buttercream over the tops of the cupcakes. Sprinkle with heart-shaped sugar sprinkles.

Tip

To ensure that you see the heart shape when you cut into the cupcakes, mark a line on the underside of each paper case. Place all the pink hearts in the same direction of the line and check the bases of the baked cupcakes before cutting.

PIÑATA PARTY CAKE

Children will love the sweetie surprise hidden inside this stunning cake and adults will marvel at how it was made! Make both cakes a day in advance so that they can firm up before you scoop.

Serves **10–12** >> ***Prep time:*** 1 hr 15 mins, plus cooling & chilling >> ***Cooking time:*** 1 hr 10 mins–1 hr 20 mins

450 g/1 lb butter, softened,
plus extra for greasing

450 g/1 lb caster sugar

8 large eggs, beaten

450 g/1 lb self-raising flour

115 g/4 oz plain flour

4 tbsp milk

280 g/10 oz mixed sweets such as
jelly babies, jelly beans and
sugar-coated chocolate drops

2 tbsp pastel-coloured confetti
sugar sprinkles

To decorate
1 quantity buttercream (see page 8)

You will also need
2 x 2-litre/3½-pint ovenproof bowls

1. Preheat the oven to 160°C/325°F/Gas Mark 3. Thoroughly grease 2 x 2-litre/3½-pint ovenproof bowls.

2. Put the butter and sugar into a large bowl and beat with a hand-held electric mixer until pale and creamy. Gradually beat in the eggs a little at a time. Sift together the self-raising flour and plain flour, then fold into the creamed mixture with the milk.

3. Divide the mixture evenly between the prepared bowls, making a dip in the centre with the back of a spoon (see step pic 3). Bake in the preheated oven for 50 minutes, then loosely cover each bowl with foil and bake for a further 20–30 minutes, or until firm to the touch and a skewer inserted into the centre of the cakes comes out clean. Leave to cool in the bowls for 10 minutes, then turn out onto a wire rack to cool completely. Wrap the cold cakes in foil and chill in the refrigerator for 4–5 hours or overnight.

4. To assemble, level the top of each cake with a serrated knife. Scoop out the centres of the cakes, leaving a 4-cm/1½-inch border (see step pic 4). Place one cake, cut-side up, on a board covered with baking paper.

5. Spread some of the buttercream around the rim of the cake and pile the sweets and half the coloured sugar sprinkles into the centre (see step pic 5). Invert the second cake on top to enclose the sweets and make a globe-shaped cake, pressing down gently to seal.

6. Using a palette knife, spread a thin layer of buttercream all over the cake to secure any loose crumbs, then chill in the refrigerator for 1 hour. Spread the remaining frosting in a thick layer over the cake and decorate with the remaining sugar sprinkles.

3

4

5

> ### Tip
> For a more colourful frosting,
> beat in a little pink or yellow
> food colouring paste with the
> buttercream.

BIRTHDAY SURPRISE GIANT CUPCAKE

Celebrate a birthday in style with this super-sized chocolate flavoured cupcake filled with a secret stash of sweets!

Serves 12 >> **Prep time:** 1 hr 10 mins, plus time to cool & chill >> **Cooking time:** 1 hr–1 hour 30 mins

40 g/1½ oz cocoa powder

5 tbsp boiling water

350 g/12 oz butter, softened, plus extra for greasing

350 g/12 oz light muscovado sugar

6 large eggs, beaten

200 g/7 oz self-raising flour, plus extra for dusting

150 g/5½ oz plain flour

To fill & decorate

1 quantity chocolate buttercream (see page 8)

icing sugar, for dusting

400 g/14 oz blue ready-to-roll icing

400 g/14 oz mixed small sweets, such as jelly beans and sugar-coated chocolate drops

You will also need

giant silicone cupcake mould

large piping bag fitted with a medium star nozzle

1. Preheat the oven to 160°C/325°F/Gas Mark 3. Thoroughly grease the base and top of a giant silicone cupcake mould, then lightly dust with flour, tipping out any excess. Place both moulds on a baking sheet. Mix the cocoa powder and water together in a small bowl to make a smooth paste and set aside.

2. Place the butter and sugar in a bowl and beat together until pale and creamy. Gradually beat in the eggs, adding a spoonful of the flour if the mixture starts to curdle. Beat in the cocoa paste, then sift in the self-raising flour and plain flour and gently fold in using a metal spoon. Divide the mixture between the prepared moulds, making a slight dip in the centre of each.

3. Bake the top cake in the preheated oven for 1 hour–1 hour 15 minutes and bake the base cake for 1 hour 20 minutes–1 hour 30 minutes, or until a skewer inserted into the centre of each cake comes out clean. Leave to cool in the moulds for 10 minutes, then turn out onto a wire rack and leave to cool completely.

4. When the cakes are cold wrap them in foil and place in the freezer for 30 minutes, or until very firm.

5. Remove the cakes from the freezer and unwrap. Level the tops of each cake with a serrated knife. Carve out a large dip in the base cake, about 10 cm/4 inches wide and 6 cm/2½ inches deep (see step pic 5).

P.T.O.

5

6

8

9

BIRTHDAY SURPRISE
GIANT CUPCAKE CONTINUED...

6. Place the base cake upside down on a board and spread a thin layer of the buttercream all over the cake. Lightly dust a surface with icing sugar and roll out the icing to a 28-cm/11-inch round. Drape the icing over the base cake, smoothing it down firmly with your fingers (see step pic 6).

7. Carefully lift up the cake and place it upright on a board or flat plate. Trim off most of the excess icing, leaving a 1-cm/½-inch border. Fold in the border over the edge of the cake.

8. Fill the dip with the sweets, reserving a few for decoration. Spread the edge of the base cake with a layer of buttercream (see step pic 8). Gently position the top cake on the base cake.

9. Spoon the remaining buttercream into a large piping bag fitted with a medium star-shaped nozzle. Pipe rosettes of buttercream all over the top of the cake to cover it completely (see step pic 9). Decorate with the remaining sweets.

Tip

If your piping skills are not so good simply swirl the chocolate buttercream over the top of the cupcake with a palette knife and decorate with your choice of sugar sprinkles.

ICE-CREAM CONE CUPCAKES

With a multi-coloured sponge inside a crisp ice cream cone these jolly cupcakes are great for a sweet treat that won't melt too quickly on a hot sunny day!

 *Makes 12* >> **Prep time:** 25 mins, plus time to cool >> **Cooking time:** 20–25 mins

12 flat-based ice-cream cones
150 g/5½ oz butter, softened
150 g/5½ oz caster sugar
3 eggs, beaten
150 g/5½ oz self-raising flour
1 tsp vanilla extract
1 tbsp milk
2 tbsp hundreds and thousands

To decorate
1 quantity buttercream
(see page 8)
12 mini chocolate flakes

- - - - - - - - - - - - - - - - - - -

You will also need
12-hole muffin tin
2 x large piping bags fitted with
a large star nozzle

1. Preheat the oven to 180°C/350°F/Gas Mark 4. Stand the ice-cream cones in a 12-hole muffin tin (see step pic 1).

2. Place the butter and sugar in a bowl and beat together until pale and creamy. Gradually beat in the eggs, adding a spoonful of the flour if the mixture starts to curdle. Sift in the flour and gently fold in using a metal spoon. Fold in the vanilla extract and milk and nearly all the hundreds and thousands (reserving 1–2 tsp for decoration).

3. Spoon the sponge mixture into a large disposable piping bag and snip off the end. Pipe the mixture into the ice-cream cones, filling each one just over half full (see step pic 3).

4. Bake in the preheated oven for 20–25 minutes, or until risen, golden and firm to the touch. Leave to cool in the tin for 10 minutes, then transfer to a wire rack and leave to cool completely.

5. To decorate, spoon the buttercream into a large piping bag fitted with a large star nozzle. Pipe peaked swirls of buttercream on top of each cupcake (see step pic 5). Push a mini chocolate flake into each swirl of buttercream and sprinkle over the reserved hundreds and thousands.

Tip

Serve these cupcakes on the day of making as the wafer cones will go soft if they are kept for too long.

1

3

5

This edition published by Parragon Books Ltd in 2014

LOVE FOOD is an imprint of Parragon Books Ltd

Parragon Books Ltd
Chartist House
15–17 Trim Street
Bath BA1 1HA, UK
www.parragon.com/lovefood

ISBN 978-1-4723-5223-1

Printed in China

Project managed by Annabel King
Designed by Karli Skelton
Recipes and home economy by Angela Drake
Edited by Fiona Biggs
Photography by Clive Streeter

Notes for the Reader
This book uses both metric and imperial measurements. Follow the same units of measurement throughout; do not mix metric and imperial. All spoon measurements are level: teaspoons are assumed to be 5 ml, and tablespoons are assumed to be 15 ml. Unless otherwise stated, milk is assumed to be full fat and eggs are medium.

Garnishes, decorations and serving suggestions are all optional and not necessarily included in the recipe ingredients or method. The times given are an approximate guide only. Preparation times differ according to the techniques used by different people and the cooking times may also vary from those given. Optional ingredients, variations or serving suggestions have not been included in the time calculations.

Picture acknowledgments
Back cover image: Cake table © Tjitske van Leeuwen Photography/Getty Images